VOICES AROUND THE MANGER

Gillian

love and blessings from

Alick & Lynn

xx

VOICES

Around the Manger

ALICK H FORD

First published in Great Britain in 2024 by Stone Monkhouse

ISBN **978-1-0683190-0-6**

Cover design by Natasha Woodcraft, with thanks to pixabay.com for images and especially Josh Willink at pexels.com

To Lynn, my dear wife who believed in me, encouraged me and gave me the time when I needed it.

Contents

Author's Note

Voices Around the Manger is neither a new translation nor a paraphrase of the Gospels, rather it is a work of fiction, or perhaps faction, in which I have tried to imagine the thoughts, words and actions of some of the main people caught up in the events and emotions of Christmas.

The basis of this work is, of course, principally the Gospels along with prophetic passages in the Old Testament. However, the 'fleshing out' comes from my imagination, guided hopefully by the Holy Spirit, and built on sixty-odd years of walking through this world with the Lord.

During lockdown (when our church weekend retreat had to be replaced by Zoom) we took part in a Christian creative writing workshop, where we were challenged to imagine how Jesus' disciples reacted to the events of the Gospels. From that, the idea of *Voices* grew, and with encouragement from my dear friend, Joy Margetts, the rest of the characters came to life.

Each portion of voice is followed by Scriptures relating to it, which may help you to reflect or meditate on the events of Christmas, and then onward from there. I hope they will encourage you to search out further gold for yourself.

I've enjoyed writing *Voices*. I hope it brings enjoyment to you as well. If it takes you a little closer to the Lord Jesus, then it was worth doing.

May the Lord bless you, keep you and bring His peace to you. To Him be the glory!

-Alick

VOICE 1

ZECHARIAH: Priest unto God

It was quite a shock, but such a marvellous surprise! This is the day I thought would never come, the day when I, Zechariah, would be called to minister the sacrifice of incense as a sweet-smelling savour to our LORD Adonai.

Hundreds of priests serve in the Temple each year. All twenty-four families, houses or courses, come along just twice a year to serve for a week at a time. Mine is the eighth, the course of Abijah, which means 'God is my Father'. I love that name. Only about fifty priests get to serve each time, to offer sacrifices and free will offerings to bless the people. They attend to the altars, fill the laver – the sanctifying water bowl for ceremonial washings – and do all the cleaning. Even then, these fifty are reduced to just six who are selected to worship in the Holy Place.

It has been such an honour and privilege to be among the called over the past thirty years. I have always tried to live righteously before the LORD Adonai in all His commandments and ordinances.

Many times I have desired to be chosen by lot to offer the incense on the altar in the Holy Place, but it just did not happen. I always tried to hide my disappointment by being pleased for the one chosen when it was not me. My congratulations echoed the times that my fellow priests would rejoice as they told me they were to have children. They would have sons to continue their line in the service of the Temple, while sadly, I had no one to follow me.

My poor Elizabeth; my dear wife. She too, is of the line of Aaron and wanted so much to give me a family, especially a son to follow me into the Temple worship. So many tears, so many false alarms, a heart broken so many times. She never blamed God or me, and I never blamed her. But, oh LORD Adonai, I would dearly love to have a son!

Today, the lots were drawn to choose who is to attend the Altar of Incense. As my name was called out by the High Priest, he drew out the white stone from his bag. I was chosen! I fell to my knees and worshipped my LORD Adonai. Many never get this honour, but now, at last, Adonai has bestowed it upon me.

Three blasts on the trumpets announce that the time has come for the evening offering. People gather at the Temple doors to pray, while I and my helpers wait at the foot of the steps, which lead from the court of the priests, to the Porch, and into the entrance of the Holy Place.

The first two mount the steps and enter, moving to the left side to attend the seven-branched golden candlestick, the Menorah. It represents the light of

God's Spirit, shining wisdom and grace into all the earth. One man carries oil to replenish the bowls, then he trims the wicks of flax. After that, the other one carries holy fire from the great Bronze Altar and lights the seven lamps. Light shines forth through the fading evening light. They withdraw, moving backwards to the steps, then join the others in the priest's Court.

The next man enters, approaching the golden table of the shewbread on the right. He removes the old shewbread, cleans the table, and then arranges the twelve new loaves upon it, each one standing for God's provision to the tribes of Israel. He too withdraws, leaving just three of us awaiting our chance to serve.

The next two enter the Holy Place, moving straight forward. They go directly to the Altar of Incense which stands as close as possible to the huge curtain separating us from the Most Holy Place – the inner room that holds the wonderful, sacred Ark of the Covenant. They remove the ashes and the burnt-out embers of the last fire. Then they put new fuel on its golden top, adding burning coals brought in a golden censor from the Brazen Altar. Only when they are satisfied that everything is exactly right can they too retire.

Now, only I stand at the foot of the stairs. I move up into the porch. I pause for a few moments, praying that I will be worthy of the faith of JEHOVAH GOD who has entrusted me with this task. I wait for the ram's horn shofar to sound the ninth hour, the time of the evening sacrifice.

-Zechariah

ECHOES

Exodus 30:1,3,6

Temple worship

'Now you shall make an altar as a place for burning incense; you shall make it of acacia wood.

You shall overlay it with pure gold, its top and its sides all around, and its horns; and you shall make a gold molding all around for it.

You shall put this altar in front of the veil that is near the ark of the testimony, in front of the mercy seat that is over the ark of the testimony, where I will meet with you.'

Psalm 141:1-2

Lord, I call upon You; hurry to me!
Listen to my voice when I call to You!
May my prayer be counted as incense before You;
The raising of my hands as the evening offering.

Ephesians 5:1-2

Therefore be imitators of God, as beloved children; and walk in love, just as Christ also loved you and gave Himself up for us, an offering and a sacrifice to God as a fragrant aroma.

VOICE 2

ZECHARIAH: Called to believe

I stand, waiting for the signal to move forward. My elation is tempered with fear. This is the supreme moment of my service in the Temple. The shofar sounds as the sun drops below the horizon. The time has come.

As I enter the Holy Place, the overwhelming peace of the presence of the LORD GOD ALMIGHTY flows over me. I know the LORD is with me.

Lit only by the candlestick, I see the Altar of Incense, beautiful in its simplicity, made of acacia wood only two cubits high, and surmounted with an ornamental tray as a crown on its top. It is just one cubit square, with the burning coals glowing red and small blue flames flickering over them. Carrying the golden bowl of incense and its golden spoon, I slowly approach the Altar. I pray that our gracious LORD will receive this offering, the prayers of righteous Israel, His chosen people, and accept our worship and praise.

As I stand before this sacred little table, only the curtain stands between me and the Ark of the Covenant.

Gently, I sprinkle the precious incense onto the coals. It crackles a little as a beautiful, intoxicating aroma rises into the air. I scatter the rest over the coals. The gorgeous perfume fills the room with its beautiful fragrance as I pray for our people:

LORD, I call upon You; hurry to me!
Listen to my voice when I call to You!
May my prayer be counted as incense before You;
The raising of my hands as the evening offering.[1]

I make a request for His favour and tender mercies on His people and pronounce the blessing for His grace to flow to us, His nation, Israel. Finally, I add a special 'Thank You' to my LORD Adonai for allowing me this gift.

I pause for a little while to take in this moment. As I turn to make my way out of the Holy Place, suddenly there appears before me a tall, handsome young man in garments of gleaming white, standing at the right side of the Altar. When I see him, I am troubled and dread flows through me. I know instinctively that this is an angel of the LORD.

He speaks to me and tells me, 'Don't be frightened, Zechariah, for GOD has listened to your prayer, and

---

[1] Psalm 141:1-2

your wife Elizabeth will give birth and give you a son. You are to call him John.'[2]

He says that John will be great, bringing joy to many. He will be a Nazarite from birth, even a forerunner of Messiah, walking in the power and spirit of Elijah.

This is such a shock that I am too overcome to believe it. I reply to the angel, 'How can I be sure it will happen? I am an old man, and my wife is getting on in years?'[3]

The angel answered him, 'I am Gabriel! I stand before the throne of GOD, in His presence. He sent me to speak to you and bring you this good news.'

I can see that he is angry!

'Look, since you did not believe my words, which will come to pass at the proper time, you will be silent, unable to speak until the day when these things will all take place because you did not believe the words I have spoken to you. They will be fulfilled!'[4]

And he left.

Trembling, I back out of the Holy Place, turn, and exit to the Court of the Priests where the people wait, wondering what has delayed my return to pronounce the final blessing on them.

As I form the words, no sound comes from my lips. It is as the angel said: I am unable to speak.

With the aid of gestures and a writing tablet, I manage to explain that an angel had appeared. I

---

[2] Luke 1:13, Author's Paraphrase

[3] Luke 1:18 Author's Paraphrase

[4] Luke 1: 19-20 Author's Paraphrase

communicate to them that GOD has promised to send us a prophet like Elijah to call many to repentance, but without implying that he will be my son. They would never believe me.

When my time of service has ended, I return to my home in the hill country of Judaea and let my dear Elizabeth know what happened. She is amazed, but she does not question the message of the angel.

And, yes, we have conceived a baby! Elizabeth has kept this miracle to herself now for five months, but she is so thrilled that her humiliation has been taken away.

I have repented of my unbelief and thanked the LORD Adonai for His wonderful gift.

My speech has not yet returned, but I am sure it will when what the angel has spoken comes to pass.

-Zechariah

ECHOES

Malachi 4:1,2,6

The Great Day of the Lord

For behold, the day is coming, burning like a furnace; and all the arrogant and every evildoer will be chaff…

But for you who fear My name, the sun of righteousness will rise with healing in its wings; You will go forth and skip about like calves from the stall.

He will turn the hearts of the fathers back to their children and the hearts of children to their fathers…

Luke 1:9b-13 (GNBUK)

The Birth Of John The Baptist Foretold

So he went into the Temple of the Lord, while the crowd of people outside prayed during the hour when the incense was burnt. An angel of the Lord appeared to him, standing on the right of the altar of where the incense was burnt. When Zechariah saw him, he was alarmed and felt afraid.

But the angel said to him, 'Don't be afraid, Zechariah! God has heard your prayer, and your wife Elizabeth will bear you a son. You are to name him John.'

VOICE 3

MARY: Betrothal

I was chatting with the other girls when a friend called, 'Mary, your mother wants you. Now!'

I made straight for home.

Though I always knew this day would come, I was still taken by surprise when I realised what the summons meant. One of my friends had received the same just a couple of weeks ago, and she was younger than me.

I got home with a fresh jar of water and found visitors in the house. There was a young man and a couple that I guessed must be his parents. My father, Eli, was in deep discussion with the older man, so I went to my mother and whispered, 'Ima, what's going on? Who are these people?'

'Hush, Mary, my child,' said Ima in a low voice. 'Jacob and Esther have come here with their son to ask us if we would let you be betrothed to Joseph. He is an honest young man, a hard worker, and he is of our clan. In fact, you are both descended from King David. Isn't that wonderful? They are trying to agree on the *'ketubah'*, you know, the marriage contract.' She straightened my tunic and tidied up my hair.

'But Ima, I'm so young. I don't think I am ready for marriage yet. Can we even afford it?' I asked her.

She replied, 'In a few days, you will have your birthday. If they can come to an agreement, you will have a whole year of betrothal to get ready. Then there is the cost of the celebration as well.'

'And the dowry?'

'Yes, Mary,' Ima added. 'It is the money that comes from the groom to your father.'

In alarm, I questioned, 'Are you and Abba selling me?'

'No, dear,' said Ima, smiling. 'That money is to help us prepare for the wedding ceremony. *Under the canopy, where husband and wife are legally united under one roof for the sake of marriage.'* [5]

'Oh, Ima! I don't know this young man. How can I marry him when I do not know him? How can I love him?'

'I did not know your abba when I was told I was to marry him,' said Ima. 'It is the custom. As I got to know him, I found him to be a good and kind husband. I grew to love him, and I still do. In any case, you do know Joseph. You two played together as little children, though he is older than you, so you may have forgotten him. He remembers you.'

'Look!' I said, noticing movement on the other side of the room. 'I think they have finished talking.'

---

[5] Mitzvah in the Talmud, part of the 613 mitzvot at Sinai. www.chabad.org

'Mary!' My father called me over to him. He took me by the hand. 'Joseph wishes to be your husband. We think you will be a good choice for him, and he for you. We will get the marriage contract written out by the Rabbi, and next week we will have the betrothal ceremony. Come, speak with him a little. We think you will like him.'

He took me over to meet Joseph then went across to Ima who was talking with Joseph's parents.

Joseph and I stood together in silence for a few moments.

I thought that at least he was quite handsome. He was shy and looked as embarrassed as I felt. He started to speak, stopped, and then tried again. 'I'm so… I'm so glad to see… you again.'

'I'm sorry,' I murmured. 'I do not remember you at all.'

'Well, you were very young then,' he added, with such kindness in his voice, I felt that maybe we could be friends after all.

His parents decided it was time to leave, so they called him. After they left, I sat down exhausted and bewildered.

The following week passed so fast. It is just a blur in my memory. Joseph and my soon-to-be relatives arrived. Our fathers read out parts of the contract, explaining that when we entered into betrothal, it was just as binding as full marriage. It was just the same, they told us, 'in all legal and religious aspects, except in cohabitation'[6]. The groom should provide for and protect me, his bride. Only after the wedding next year could we become one flesh.

Joseph now had to formally request if I would be his bride. I was asked whether I consented.

How could I say no? Everything had been agreed. Carried along by the moment, and in obedience to my abba, I consented.

My father poured a cup of wine. 'Blessed art Thou, O LORD our God, King of the world, who sanctified Israel by wedding and betrothal.'[7]

He handed the cup to Joseph, who took a drink and handed it to me. I hesitated for a moment, then I took a sip.

Then, everyone looked to Joseph as he declared, *'You are my wife whom I have betrothed. You are consecrated to me according to the Law of Moses and Israel.'*[8]

Joseph tentatively held out his open right hand to me. Trembling, I reached out and slid my hand into his. We gently held hands. A strange peace came upon me as I realised this was the first step to us becoming one.

A blessing was spoken over us, and everyone clapped. We were betrothed!

-Mary

---

[6] Mitzvah in the Talmud, part of the 613 mitzvot at Sinai. www.chabad.org

[7] ibid

[8] ibid

ECHOES

Proverbs 19:14

House and wealth are an inheritance from fathers,
  But a prudent wife is from the LORD.

Psalm128:3

Your wife shall be like a fruitful vine within your house,
Your children like olive plants around your table.

Proverbs 31:10-12 and 28-30

An excellent wife, who can find?
For her worth is far above jewels.
The heart of her husband trusts in her,
And he will have no lack of gain.
She does him good and not evil
All the days of her life.

Her children rise up and bless her,
Her husband also, and he praises her, saying:
'Many daughters have done nobly,
But you excel them all.'
Charm is deceitful and beauty is vain,
But a woman who fears the LORD, she shall be praised.

VOICE 4

MARY: Chosen of God

A few weeks passed by while I came to terms with my new status. Joseph was away, not just doing his work as a carpenter, but starting to build us a new house. My birthday went by almost unnoticed, as I collected the things that I would need to set up home. Ima taught me how to organize my day, so I could do all the extra tasks that would have to be done. I thought I already knew quite a lot, but there was so much more.

I knew how to grind wheat and knead dough, but to heat and use an oven for baking was a new skill I had to learn. Sewing was no longer a child's pastime. No, now it had to include making and repairing clothes and blankets. Before, I would just fetch water, but I did not have to wash the floors, clean the house, or make sure there was water to drink while it was still cool. I began to wonder, did I really want to be married if it took so much work and time?

The thoughts that every Jewish maiden dreams of went through my imagination. Who would the LORD God choose as the one to fulfil the promise of Isaiah:

> Behold, a virgin will be with child and shall bear a son, and she will call his name Immanuel?[9]

In less than a year it will be too late for me. Still, it would have been nice to be the one!

The idea was hardly in my mind when something strange took place. The room seemed to become full of light as if the sun was in the house. I called out in alarm, 'Ima, Abba, is that you?'

No answer!

Then, into the brightness, stepped a tall young man of great beauty, his face framed by white hair, and his white garments glowing with light. I knew instinctively that this was an angel. I was puzzled and frightened by his words when he said,

> Greetings highly favoured one. The LORD is with you. Do not be afraid, Mary, for you have found favour with God.
>
> Behold, you will conceive in your womb and bear a son, and you shall name Him Jesus.
>
> He will be great, and He will be called the Son of the Most High; and the LORD God will give to him the throne of His father, David.
>
> He will reign over the house of Jacob forever, and there will be no end to His kingdom.[10]

I could hardly take it in. I said to him, 'How can this be since I am a maiden?'

---

[9] Isaiah 7:14 Paraphrased

[10] Luke 1:30-33 Author's Paraphrase

The angel answered me,

> God's Holy Spirit will come upon you, so that the power of the Most High will cover you with His shadow. The Child will be holy and will be called the Son of God.
> And I can tell you this: your cousin Elizabeth also, in her old age, has conceived a son. She was said to be barren, but now she is in her sixth month, for nothing is impossible to God.[11]

'I am the LORD's handmaiden,' I replied. 'May it happen to me just as you have said.'

The angel smiled joyfully, and in a moment, he was gone, and the brightness slowly faded away.

Overcome by the weight of this visit, I went to my private area and closed the curtain about me. As I sat on the bed, still in a state of amazement, I realized that there seemed to be a gentle breeze blowing through the room as a glistening cloud formed and shone all around me. A beautiful perfume filled the air, like the scent of a thousand flowers, while the cloud grew deeper, quietly wrapping itself around me like a warm blanket.

I thought that I heard soft music playing, just like David would have played on the hillside, and I gently drifted off into sleep.

It was very early the next morning when I awoke. I did not want to disturb my parents, so I lay quietly as I tried

---

[11] Luke 1:35 -37 Author's Paraphrase

to make sense of what had happened. I was to give birth to a son! Not just any son, but the Messiah Himself! How could I tell them? I knew in my own heart that it was true, but would they believe me when I told them?

What was I to do now? Then I remembered what the angel had said about Elizabeth. I made up my mind to visit her at her home in Ein Kerem, in the hill country of Judaea, as soon as I could.

I would tell no one else until I had shared it with her. She would understand!

-Mary

ECHOES

Isaiah 7:14

Therefore the Lord Himself will give you a sign: Behold, the virgin will conceive and give birth to a son, and she will name Him Immanuel [*God with us*].

Galatians 4:4–5

But when the fullness of the time came, God sent His Son, born of a woman, born under the Law, so that He might redeem those who were under the Law, that we might receive the adoption as sons *and daughters*.

Luke 1:30,31

And the angel said to her, 'Do not be afraid, Mary, for you have found favour with God. And behold, you will conceive in your womb and give birth to a son, and you shall name him Jesus.'[12]

---

[12] Greek: 'Iesous'. Hebrew: 'Yehoshua' translated 'Joshua' in Old Testament, meaning 'Jehovah is salvation'

John 1:14

And the Word became flesh and dwelt among us,
and we saw His glory,
glory as of the only begotten from the Father,
full of grace and truth.

VOICE 5

ELIZABETH: A Trip to Ein Kerem

It is so amazing that the LORD Adonai should grant me, Elizabeth, such a wonderful gift – so good to be expecting a child at last, after all the years of hurt and discrimination.

It's hard to believe that it's already six months since we conceived him. Even now, I am not too old to raise a son, at least until he reaches adulthood. Then he will have to look after me and Zechariah for the few years we will have left, or until he enters into his calling.

Sitting outside, looking over towards Jerusalem, I think what a lovely place this is to raise a child. Ein Kerem is so delightful with its white limestone reflecting the sunlight and its pink sandstone buildings. It is called 'The Vineyard of the Spring' for good reason.

We have the cypress trees for shade and the crops of olives and grapes that make it so lovely. I'm sure John will love it. The LORD Adonai told my husband that John would go before the Messiah, in the spirit of Elijah, to call the people to repentance and prepare them for His coming. I wonder if the Messiah is already here, or if He is yet to be born? We just don't know. God will reveal that to us in His good time, so we have to be patient, watch and do our part.

But it would be nice to know. There are still many devout people looking for His time, maybe like that caravan of wagons going through Ein Kerem towards Jerusalem. Unusually, it has paused. Someone is getting down and saying goodbye to them. Strange. Still, I must go in and check if that yeast has done its job. Then I need to set up the oven, ready to bake the bread.

As I stand awkwardly to go indoors, I hear a voice calling. It is the young woman from the caravan. 'Elizabeth, Shalom!'

It is my cousin, Mary. At the sound of Mary's voice, the baby inside me leaps. Immediately, I am filled with the Holy Spirit and cry out, 'Mary, you are so blessed above all other women! The child that you are carrying is the most blessed of all! I am so honoured, that the mother of my Lord has come to visit me.'

'But, how do you know, Elizabeth? It does not even show yet?'

'As soon as I heard your greeting, the baby within me jumped with gladness. The Holy Spirit came upon me, revealing who you are and the One you are carrying. You are so faithful to believe that what the LORD has promised to you will come true!'

The Spirit of God comes upon Mary too and she declares,

> My soul glorifies the LORD, and my spirit rejoices in God my Saviour, for He has been mindful of the humble state of His servant.
> From now on all generations will call me blessed, because the Mighty One has done great things for me – Holy is His Name.
> His mercy extends to those who fear Him from generation to generation.[13]

By this time, I am on my knees worshipping the LORD our God. If only Zechariah was here now instead of serving in the Temple. How he would love this moment.

Mary continues,

> God has performed mighty deeds with His arm
> and scattered those who are proud in their
> inmost thoughts.
> He has brought down rulers from their thrones
> but has lifted up the humble.
> He has filled the hungry with good things but
> sent the rich away empty.
> He has helped His servant Israel, remembering
> to be merciful to Abraham and his descendants
> forever, even as He said to our fathers.[14]

After she finishes speaking, she helps me to my feet and we throw our arms around each other – laughing, crying, dancing. We embrace again. Such joy, such

---

[13] Luke 1:46 -50 paraphrase

[14] Luke 1:51-55 paraphrase

wonder! We praise our LORD Adonai, yelling with happiness.

Then, as the neighbours start gathering to see what is going on, I decide I should take Mary into the house. 'I think I had better sit down and get my breath back while you tell me all about it, Mary. I want to hear everything right from the start. I must know how it has happened.'

Mary gets cups of water for us and starts her story. She tells me how she met Joseph, how they were betrothed, and how they had started to prepare for their future marriage. Then she discloses the visit by the Angel Gabriel and his announcement that she had been chosen to bear the Christ-Child whose name is to be Jesus. She explains to me how the Holy Spirit came to her and how the baby was conceived.

However, she decided to keep it all secret, even from her parents and Joseph, until she had been to see us to ask what she should do now. She is so relieved to see that the word of the angel to Zechariah has come to pass. It is such a comfort to her, in place of the fear that she had dreamt it all. My belly is proof enough!

When Zechariah gets back from the Temple, Mary has to tell her story all over again. He is so thrilled that he dances around the room, but he still cannot speak.

Mary stays with us for a while. At first, there is nothing to prove that she is pregnant, but soon, she starts to get backache and is very tired. Once Mary has been with us for over two months, I can tell that she is getting a bit restless. She knows she must go home and is nervous about telling her people what has happened. Sickness in the morning has more or less stopped, and she is just beginning to show.

She came to us this morning to say that she can't put it off anymore. It is time she went back to Nazareth, especially to tell Joseph the marvellous news. Oh! If only he will believe her.

I'm so sorry she will not be here for the birth of my John. Maybe it's better that way. Still, I will miss her. I do hope we shall be able to see little Jesus when He comes. Wouldn't it be wonderful if He and John became friends and played together?

Zechariah has made arrangements for Mary to travel home along with some relatives he trusts. I know that the LORD will take care of her when I think of the One she is carrying.

When she leaves, I am sure to cry. She is certain to face opposition and danger when she gets home, so I will pray for her safety and especially for her son, just like the way she is praying for my safe delivery in just a few weeks' time!

-Elizabeth

ECHOES

Luke 1:39–45 (GNBUK)

Elizabeth's greeting

Mary got ready and hurried off to a town in the hill country of Judaea. She went into Zechariah's house and greeted Elizabeth. When Elizabeth heard Mary's greeting, the baby moved within her. Elizabeth was filled with the Holy Spirit, and she sang with a loud voice, 'You are the most blessed of all women, and blessed is the child you will bear! Why should this great thing happen to me, that my Lord's mother comes to visit me? For as soon as I heard your greeting, the baby within me jumped with gladness. How happy you are to believe that the Lord's message to you will come true!'

Luke 1:46-55

The Magnificat

And Mary said:

'My soul exalts the Lord,
And my spirit has rejoiced in God my Saviour.
For He has had regard for the humble state of His bond-servant;
For behold, from now on all generations will call me blessed.
For the Mighty One has done great things for me;
And holy is His name.
And His mercy is to generation after generation.
Toward those who fear Him.'

VOICE 6

JOSEPH: Husband and Father

'Oh, Joseph!' Mary looked distraught. 'Whatever are we going to do?'

'It's going to be alright, Mary,' I replied. 'I'm so sorry! I should have trusted you when you came back from visiting Elizabeth. When you told me all about how you came to be with child, it seemed such an incredible tale that I thought it could not possibly be true.'

She stared at me in alarm as I continued, 'I thought you had been unfaithful to me. I could not believe that you had betrayed me like that, and then made up such an excuse. I thought, how could she blame the LORD? It's ridiculous! No one has ever heard of such a thing before.

'I thought then about what I should do. If I denounced you publicly, you would have been disgraced in front of everyone. You would have been judged as having committed adultery. It could even have resulted in you being stoned to death! I would never do that to you. I love you so much, but it hurt so badly when I thought that you had been with someone else.

'I thought I could no longer go through with the marriage ceremony, so I decided to break the betrothal and divorce you quietly. Your mother and father could not believe your story either, but they said they would let you live with them, although they thought your life in Nazareth would be very difficult. We even wondered if you could go to live with your relatives in Ein Kerem. No one knows you there.'

Mary tried to speak, but the words refused to come. Tears rolled silently down her cheeks.

'Please don't cry, Mary. Don't be frightened.' I took her hand in mine. 'You don't have to say anything. Please let me explain. Last night, after I made up my mind to divorce you, I had a strange dream. The Angel of the LORD Adonai appeared to me. He spoke to me gently but with great authority. He said,

> Joseph, son of David, do not be afraid to take Mary home as your wife. It is by the Holy Spirit that she has conceived. She will have a Son, and you must name him Jesus because He will save his people from their sins.[15]

'When I woke up, I remembered what was written in the Scroll of Isaiah:

> Look! A virgin is with child and will give birth to a son. He will be called Immanuel. *God with us.*[16]

---

[15] Matthew 1:20,21 paraphrased

[16] Isaiah 7:14, paraphrased

'How happy you are to believe the Lord's message to you. Now I know that everything you told me is true! Come with me to our home. Be my wife! Yes, we must still stay pure until after your child is born. Then, I will adopt him as my own son, and we will name Him Jesus, just as the angel said.'

Mary could not be silent any longer. She praised the LORD Adonai. Throwing her arms around me, she wept, this time with joy. Then we gave thanks to our LORD and praised Him together for His grace to us.

We set up home in my new house in Nazareth. People had made up their minds that the baby must have been mine, so I gave up trying to tell them the truth.

Things started to come together for us as the months passed. My carpentry business grew so that a little money began coming in. The time when the baby would be born was getting close. While Mary made baby clothes, I made a wooden cradle 'fit for a king'. We even informed our Rabbi to get ready to admit our son into the covenant of Abraham. When he questioned how we could be so sure the baby would be a boy, we just smiled and said, 'Trust us, we know!'

Then, out of the blue, there came an edict from Caesar Augustus – a census of the whole Roman Empire was to be made. Everybody had to go back to their tribal city to be counted. For us, that was Bethlehem, the city of our ancestor, David.

It was at least a five-day journey from Nazareth to Bethlehem, just south of Jerusalem, and Mary was due to give birth almost any time.

I made enquiries to see if she could be registered in Nazareth, but no, she had to go. Thank You, LORD, that we had a donkey! He may have been old, but he still had one last big job before he retired.

-Joseph

ECHOES

Isaiah 7:14

Therefore, the Lord Himself will give you a sign: Behold, the virgin will conceive and give birth to a son, and she will name Him Immanuel.

Isaiah 9:6

For a child will be born to us, a son will be given to us; and the government will rest on His shoulders; and His name will be called Wonderful Counsellor, Mighty God, Eternal Father, Prince of Peace.

Ezekiel 37:24, 26-27

My servant David will be king over them, and they will all have one shepherd; and they will walk in My ordinances and keep My statutes and follow them.

...I will make a covenant of peace with them; it will be an everlasting covenant with them. And I will place them and multiply them and set My sanctuary in their midst forever. My dwelling place also will be among them, and I will be their God, and they will be My people.

VOICE 7

JOSEPH: Protector

For safety, our parents and our other relatives decided to travel to Bethlehem together. Although some of them were still uneasy about us, they agreed to let us join them. They made room for Mary in one of the wagons, with the donkey tethered behind carrying food, warm blankets, and things for the birth of Jesus. I had to walk most of the way.

We left on the first day of the week to give us six days to get there, so avoiding Shabbat. Skirting Mount Tabor, we went east through the Valley of Jezreel with its fig, olive and date palm trees, which gave shade and even some food. We chose to cross the River Jordan to avoid travelling through Samaria. Jews are not welcome there.

We followed the east bank, travelling south to the crossing near Bethany-Beyond-Jordan, hoping the river was not too high, as the crossing can be quite difficult.

The first couple of days went well, although the jolting of the cart was not pleasant for Mary. After a while, it caused leg cramps and pressure on her back and stomach. She found that walking was a little better, or riding on the donkey for a while. Most of all, she was just so tired. We realized that we were holding the others back, so on the third morning we told the party to go on ahead while we made our own way more slowly. Mary's mother, Anna, wanted to stay with us, but Eli managed to persuade her that it was not a sensible idea because her walking was not good. Reluctantly she gave in and went with the others, saying she would try to find a guest room for us in Bethlehem.

It was not as easy from there on, as the grassy paths gradually gave way to sandy and then more rocky tracks, while the heat of the day increased as we followed the river lower and lower. I think we must have been below the level of the Great Sea by that time. It seemed cooler in the night, but happily, sometimes there were booths left by other travellers which we were able to use. I was amazed at Mary's strength and determination. She really is very special!

It was the sixth day when we reached the crossing. We decided to try and cross before the sun went down, and then we could rest for Shabbat. The rains had not come yet, and the Jordan was low, so we waded into the river with Mary on the donkey.

I tried to find the shallowest path across, but even then, I needed to steady the donkey whenever he missed his footing or stumbled. Mary nearly took a fall a couple of times, yet with the LORD's help, we made it. I aided some other travellers by mending their damaged handcart before nightfall, so they shared some of their food with us. It was good to take a day's rest before facing the section of dry ridges through the rocky Judaean desert.

On the first day of the week, somewhat refreshed, we started the arduous journey to Jerusalem, taking as much water with us as we could carry. We passed through Jericho and remembered where our ancestor Rahab survived the walls falling down, then later married Salmon to become the great-great-grandmother of King David.

Next, we faced the hardest part – climbing up and over the arid desert pass. By the time we reached the descent to Jerusalem, Mary was so tired that we spent the night there. As we looked towards Bethlehem, beyond the city, it seemed like the brightest star we had ever seen sat over it, almost as if showing us the way.

The road down was difficult. Our lovely old donkey was magnificent. Even so, it took much longer to reach the city than we had expected.

Mary was starting to get tightening pains.

Half the day had gone before we passed through the south of Jerusalem and commenced the last few hours to Bethlehem. Mary's pains were closer together by the time we got there. It was almost dark, and we had nowhere to stay. We asked if anyone knew whether Anna and Eli had been able to find us lodgings. They had, but as we did not arrive in time, they were let to others.

Mary's waters broke, and she cried out in pain. Desperate, I knocked on every door, to no avail. Then an innkeeper said that we could use his stable if we could put up with the animals. We would accept anything! Behind the house was a barn built on to a cave. He moved some animals into stalls to clear a space for us, while I put down straw and threw the donkey's rugs over it for Mary to lie down.

I did what I could to help, but Mary did all the hard work instinctively. It was not long before I heard the cries of a baby. This world is a cold place outside the warmth of His mother's womb! We washed Him in water, cut the cord, rubbed Him with salt and wrapped Him in warm woollen cloths. Mary lifted Him to her bosom to feed her son for the first time.

Jesus was born!

Once the baby was satisfied, we carefully wrapped Him in strips of linen on which Mary had embroidered the lion of Judah, showing that he is of our tribe. Then, we put Him into the carved stone manger, which I had lined with hay and a woollen blanket. He would be safe there. He was soon sleeping contentedly.

Even the animals were quiet, when suddenly, the door opened, and the scruffy head of a shepherd peered in. He was carrying a lamb.

'Is this where the newborn baby lies?' the shepherd asked.

'Yes,' I replied, 'But how did you know?'

'The angel told us to come and see the Messiah, our Saviour. He said to go to David's town to find the baby. And that He would be lying in a manger, wrapped in swaddling bands. May we come in?'

Mary roused herself, smiled and beckoned them in. They gazed in wonder at baby Jesus and praised the

LORD Adonai. As the baby stirred and opened His eyes, they dropped to their knees and worshipped Him.

Then they told us how, when the angel had announced the birth of Jesus, the sky was suddenly flooded with light, and heaven went wild, full of angels, shouting, 'Glory to God!' and 'Peace on earth!'

So, we asked the blessing of our LORD Adonai to be upon them and wished them well, as they went on their way full of wonder and adoration at God's grace to His people. We could hear them for a while, telling everyone they met that the Messiah had been born.

Jesus was again sleeping happily; Mary and I were exhausted, and I soon fell asleep. Mary said later that she dozed a little, but lay, turning the things we had experienced over and over in her heart, treasuring all the wonderful things that had happened.

How was it possible? She had given birth to the Messiah!

-Joseph

ECHOES

Luke 2:6–7

While they, [Joseph and Mary], were there [in Bethlehem], the time came for her to give birth. And she gave birth to her firstborn son; and she wrapped Him in cloths, and laid Him in a manger, because there was no room for them in the inn.

John 1:1,11–13 (GNBUK)

In the beginning the Word already existed; the Word was with God, and the Word was God.

He came to his own country, but his own people did not receive him. Some, however, did receive him and believed in him; so he gave them the right to become God's children... God himself was their Father.

Luke 2: 8–15

In the same region, there were some shepherds staying out in the fields and keeping watch over their flock at night. And an angel of the Lord suddenly stood near them, and the glory of the Lord shone around them; and they were terribly frightened.

And so the angel said to them, 'Do not be afraid; for behold, I bring you good news of great joy which will be for all the people; for today in the city of David there has been born for you a Savior, who is Christ the Lord. And this will be a sign for you: you will find a baby wrapped in cloths and lying in a manger.'

And suddenly there appeared with the angel a heavenly army of angels praising God and saying, 'Glory to God in the highest, And on earth peace among people with whom He is pleased.'

When the angels had departed from them into heaven, the shepherds began saying to one another, 'Let's go straight to Bethlehem, then, and see this thing that has happened, which the Lord has made known to us.'

VOICE 8

MARY: A Visit to the Temple

Early the next morning, Jesus woke us. He might be the Coming One, but He is still a real baby, wanting to be fed and changed. Word of my new baby soon got around, so Abba and Ima came looking for us. About the third hour, they found our stable. At first, they were horrified that their daughter had given birth in such a place, even though the animals had been taken out to pasture by that time. Yet once my parents saw Jesus, they forgot about the place and were captivated by Him.

Soon, Joseph's parents sought out our little shelter as well. They had found it difficult to believe that Jesus was conceived by the Holy Spirit. They came in warily and a bit unsure, especially toward me.

Then they saw Jesus. Immediately, they were cooing and fussing over Him. Joseph and I caught each other's eye and could not help smiling a little, as the two grandmothers vied with each other to hold Him. Both wanted Him to themselves. After a little while, when I saw that He had had enough, I took Jesus back and said it was time for His next feed. Joseph suggested they all left me in private for a while, so they took the opportunity to find out where the census was being taken.

Everyone had to appear personally to be registered. Of course, there was a payment to be made which took most of our remaining funds. Imagine my surprise when Joseph returned with a Roman guard and a clerk, who had to see us for themselves, to be sure we existed. Satisfied, they quickly left; glad to be out of a smelly stable.

There were still no rooms available for us. Our families had crammed into some that already had other travellers in them. We could have shared too, but in a funny way, we were glad to have the more peaceful stable to ourselves. Even sharing with the animals helped to keep us warm at night.

King David certainly had a lot of descendants! No doubt, in a few days, rooms would be freed as many people would start to go back to their homes. In any case, we had very little money for a proper room, let alone for food and supplies for our baby. Some of the Bethlehem folk were very kind to us, giving us help and little gifts, even though many were quite as poor as us, bless them.

Joseph mended someone's door, so as news that he was a carpenter and stonemason got about, he began getting work in and around the town, earning payments sometimes in cash, but mostly in kind.

I was legally unclean for seven days, just as in my monthly time, so I was confined to the stable. On the eighth day, our parents and some other relatives came to us, along with the local Rabbi, for the circumcision of Jesus. He cried of course, but we all rejoiced that He was now brought into the Holy Covenant between the LORD God Adonai and our forefather, Abraham.

The next day our relatives started back for home. They blessed us, gave us what spare money they could afford, and then they kissed us, especially baby Jesus. They left for home with an exciting tale to tell. There was lots of laughter and tears as they said goodbye.

As Joseph got paid for more work, and with the money we had been given, we were able to move up into the house above the stable. A room was now empty as many of the visitors to Bethlehem had been registered, paid their taxes, and wanted to be off.

We had to stay in Bethlehem for at least thirty-three days for me to be purified from my bleeding. Only then could we go to the priest at the Temple Sanctuary to do as the Law commanded by bringing a lamb, or two doves, as a sin offering and a burnt offering, for every first-born male is called holy to the LORD.[17]

When the time came, we could only manage a pair of pigeons. It was fine, however. The priest received them generously as he looked kindly on our little son, making the presentation as if we had brought the best lamb in the flock. God will reward him, I am sure.

Something wonderful and unexpected happened next. As we entered the Temple Porch, a man full of years came up to us, saying that the Holy Spirit had

---

[17] See Exodus 4:20

revealed to him that he would not die until he had seen the LORD's promised Messiah.

This good and God-fearing man, whose name was Simeon, took Jesus up in his arms, gave thanks to God and amazed both of us as he spoke by the power of the Spirit:

> LORD Adonai, now You may release Your bond servant to die in Your peace, just as You said.
> I have seen with my own eyes Your bringer of salvation
> Whom You have made ready in the sight of all peoples.
> Light to bring revelation to the Gentile nations,
> And glory to Your own people Israel.[18]

This gracious man then blessed us both, and turning to Mary, said,

> Be aware, this child is set to cause the disastrous fall of many, and the raising to resurrection life for others in Israel. He will be a miraculous sign that will be denied, even to the point where sorrow, like a sharp sword, will go through your own soul. Yet the deepest thoughts of many hearts will be revealed.[19]

Then he slipped away into the crowd. What could it mean?

---

[18] Luke 2:29-32, Author's paraphrase

[19] Luke 2:34-35, paraphrase

We had hardly recovered when a very old lady came up to us. She was Anna, of the tribe of Asher, a lady of great grace and devotion. We found out later that she had only been married for seven years when she had lost her husband, and since then, she never left the Temple. At the age of eighty-four, she was still worshipping God day and night, with fasting and prayer.

Now, untainted by the spirit of the age, she came up to us, led by the Holy Spirit. She saw Jesus. Bending down, she stooped in kindness, worshipping God for letting her see her Messiah who was now revealed to her aged eyes by the LORD Adonai.

She gave thanks to God for the One who would set His people free. After she had blessed Him, she went away with a new anointing upon her life for her remaining years. She told everyone about Him, saying that our Messiah had been born – He who would redeem Israel and set Jerusalem free. We left the Temple thrilled, excited, yet quite confused.

We found our way to where we had left our donkey, paid the man who looked after him and made our way back to Bethlehem. Jesus and I were very tired by the time we got back to the house. Joseph had a few more jobs to finish, so he decided we would not set off for home until we were all stronger and more rested. It was as well that we stayed a little longer, for God had another surprise for us.

-Mary, with Simeon and Anna

ECHOES

Luke 2:29- 32

Now, Lord, You are letting Your bond-servant depart in peace,
According to Your word;
For my eyes have seen Your salvation,
Which You have prepared in the presence of all the peoples:
A light for revelation for the Gentiles,
And the glory of Your people Israel.

Luke 2:36-38 (GNBUK)

There was a very old prophetess, a widow named Anna, the daughter of Phanuel of the tribe of Asher. She had been married for only seven years and was now eighty-four years old. She never left the Temple; day and night she worshipped God, fasting and praying.

That very same hour she arrived and gave thanks to God and spoke about the child to all who were waiting for God to set Jerusalem free.

VOICE 9

JOSEPH: Unexpected visitors

'Abba,' said Jesus, 'tell me the story about the wise men who came to Bethlehem.'

'Yes, of course,' I replied. 'But you have heard it lots of times. You must know it by heart.'

'Ah, but you tell it so well, and you often add extra bits I haven't heard before. And it is one of my favourites,' said Jesus.

I gave in to my son's pleas and laid down my tools. 'After we had been to the Temple in Jerusalem, we went back to Bethlehem,' I said. 'We had a proper room by then, because many of the people of the House of David had registered, paid their taxes and gone back to their homes. Having our own little room made it so much better for your mother, even if it did cost us a little more.'

'Oh yes, I remember. You were starting to get carpentry work by then and people were paying you what they could manage. I'm sure you did lots of it for free,' Jesus added.

'How do you know that?' I said, a bit surprised.

'Ima told me,' he replied, chuckling. 'She was so proud of you! You always had food for us, and all the other things we needed. Will you teach me to be a carpenter?'

'Yes, when you are a bit older and can handle the tools safely. Some are very sharp.' I returned to the story:

> In Bethlehem, we had lots of visitors at first who came to see you. There were shepherds, relatives and local people who were wanting to see you as well. I would have stopped them, but Mary said not to, because they wanted to see the child born to be their Saviour.
>
> It was just a little while after we returned from the Temple that we had another visit. It was well into the night. The sun had been down for some hours and everywhere was quiet, until we heard voices and banging on doors out in the city square. It was quite a racket – not just men shouting, but saddlebags clattering and animals grunting and snorting. For they had camels, and not a few. As I peered out, I saw some riders holding blazing torches. Others were clearly warriors to guard the leading men in the group. Folk came out of their homes, rubbing their eyes, to see the spectacle.
>
> 'Where is He who has been born King of the Jews?' demanded one of the riders.
>
> 'There is a newborn baby boy in that inn over there,' called out a neighbour.

A soldier handed his torch to a servant who ran into the courtyard and roused the landlord.

'Where is the child?' he demanded.

'In the upper room.' The innkeeper brought him to our door. 'Quietly, He may be asleep.'

I opened the door to him, and as he looked in and saw you asleep, he stood transfixed for a moment.

He whispered, 'Oh yes,' then turning, he ran back to tell the others. 'My lords. He is here!'

There was a flurry of activity as the camels knelt down, and the three main riders dismounted. They took off their duster cloaks, smartened up their appearance, and then went to their saddlebags to retrieve small cases wrapped in cloths and oilskins. They each handed the elaborate boxes to their personal servants and, telling them to follow, they came into the inn.

Coming up to our door, they asked gently, 'May we come in and see the Holy Child?'

These were surely dignitaries from far away. Dressed in magnificent garments edged with gold, and silks in colours I had never seen before. They were arrayed with jewel-encrusted ornaments and turbans of the distant east. Overawed, I waved them in. They bowed to me as I brought them to see you. Your mother picked you up out of your bed. She smiled at them and held you on her lap to let them see you.

They said nothing, just dropped to their knees. They started worshipping you in languages that I did not understand. After a little while, they switched to Aramaic to explain that they had gifts to present to you. Gifts most fitting for you, the Saviour born to be King of the Jews.

The first one gestured to his servant, who stood a little distance behind him. He brought forward an ornately carved box, which he carefully placed in his master's hands. It was obviously rather heavy.

The stranger moved a little closer. He opened it slowly and inclined it towards you, saying, 'This is my gift to You. It is gold, the most precious gold of Ophir. It is the only gift worthy of You, for You are the true King of the Jews. Indeed, You are the High King of earth and heaven. I now call You my King. I worship You.' With that, he bowed down with his face to the ground.

The second stranger came forward to join his companion. Taking his decorated box, he showed its contents to you. The perfume of the amber-coloured beads of resin from the torchwood tree filled the air. 'I bring my present to You, the one true priest who stands above all other servants of the God of heaven. I bring You frankincense, to declare You as pure and good, the only one worthy to stand and bring the prayers of all who call on God for salvation. As this aroma rises to heaven, so Your mediation alone is heard beyond the stars. I now make You my priest forever.' He too bowed his face to the ground to pray in his strange language.

The last visitor hesitated for a moment before he came forward. His black ebony box was plain, and as he opened it, a sharper, more pungent scent came forth. It was myrrh, the lifeblood of the thorn trees of Cush, used for embalming the dead. The small flask of distilled dark brown sap must have cost a fortune.

'This, my gift,' he said quietly, 'is for the One, the only, perfect sacrifice for all our sins. It speaks of suffering, death and burial. Only the sinless life will do, so this offering speaks of You. I worship You, Son of God!' Bowing to the ground, he mixed his adoration with his tears.

After a little while, all three were quiet, stood, placed their gifts before you, and withdrew toward the door.

'Please,' I called out. 'You cannot just leave us. Stay, your honours. At least take some refreshment with us and you can tell us how you came to find us.'

-Joseph

ECHOES

Sleep Little Jesus

Still and thoughtful, Mary watches
Christ, the infant, quietly sleeping,
Ponders in her inmost being
Secrets she alone is keeping.

How can He who formed the heavens,
Created earth by His commands,
Be the tiny helpless baby
She now cradles in her hands?

Yet the angels bowed down to Him,
Songs of heaven rang through the sky,
Wise men brought their precious presents,
Wondering shepherds gathered nigh.

For this little child of favour
By His word all things sustains.
Brightness of the Father's glory
Brings us peace that grace obtains.

To reign at last at God's right hand
And take the place that he has won,
To rule throughout eternal years
As King of Kings and God's own Son.

But first, a sword shall pierce her heart,
When sin and curse will be undone.
Until that fateful day is here –
Sleep, Little Jesus, Mary's son.

Alick H Ford, 2021

Matthew 2:1–2, 6, 10–11

Now after Jesus was born in Bethlehem of Judea in the days of Herod the king, behold, magi from the east arrived in Jerusalem, saying, 'Where is He who has been born King of the Jews? For we saw His star in the east and have come to worship Him.'

> And you, Bethlehem, land of Judah,
> Are by no means least among the leaders of Judah;
> For from you shall come forth a ruler
> Who will shepherd My people Israel.

When they saw the star, they rejoiced exceedingly with great joy. And after they came into the house, they saw the Child with His mother Mary; and they fell down and worshiped Him. Then they opened their treasures and presented to Him gifts of gold, frankincense and myrrh.

Isaiah 60:1,3

Arise, shine; for your light has come,
And the glory of the LORD has risen upon you.
Nations will come to your light,
And kings to the brightness of your rising.

VOICE 10

THE MAGI: Rejoicing in their King

When the Christ child's parents asked us to stay, I, Melchior, replied on behalf of us all. 'Thank you. That would be wonderful. We have lots of food and wine which we can share with you.'

Within minutes, our servants set out a feast for us, while we Magi, most unexpected visitors, each took a turn holding Jesus. How our faces glowed with awe and delight. Eventually, seeing that He was tiring, Mary gently took Him from us to put Him back into His bed. He was asleep as soon as He lay down.

As we all reclined around the food, Joseph gave thanks, amazed at the splendour of it.

'Herod provided most of this,' said Casper. 'He wanted to impress us with his generosity. He is a strange and dangerous man. He built the Temple, palaces, and fortresses, and he killed his wife, sons, and anyone else who may challenge his position. I fear he is not to be trusted.'

'I am sorry we alerted him of the birth of your son,' I said. 'But he was adamant that we return to inform him where Jesus was, so that he too may come and worship Him.'

'But, how did you learn of Jesus?' asked Mary. 'There in the East, where our people were once exiled?'

'It started when we saw a new star in the far eastern sky, slowly moving to the west,' said Casper.

'We are Magi,' interrupted Balthazar. 'We study the heavens to interpret the times, seasons and future events. A new star is extremely unusual.'

Casper continued, 'There was no doubt. The heavens do not make mistakes. Something prodigious was about to happen! We studied old writings, the prophecies of Daniel, Isaiah and others. We watched the progress of the stars. There was a conjunction of the King, the Maiden and the new star which came together in the constellation of the Lion – that's Judah! Surely the time was upon us for the arrival of the King of the Jews. We believe He is the new King of Judah and the Messiah for all the world. So, we followed the star, and it brought us to Jerusalem. There we enquired of Herod, but he knew nothing of it.'

I interjected disdainfully, 'He asked his religious advisors. They had no answer until they searched out Micah's words about Bethlehem. They didn't even know their own Scriptures!'

Casper concluded, 'Outside the palace, we saw that the star had moved on. We followed it until it rested above this place. So, here we are, and there He is! How gracious is God Most High, that we should be allowed to see the Saviour of humankind!'

We talked long into the night until sleep overcame us all. Several times, Jesus needed attention, of course. When morning came, we prepared to leave. We had one more look at the son of Mary, the Child born to be King.

Before we left, we whispered to Joseph and Mary that the LORD Adonai had warned us in a dream not to go back to Herod, but to go home by a different route. In obedience, we chose to do so. Reluctantly, we mounted our camels. Those beautiful parents blessed us and bade us godspeed.

We said our fond farewells and rode away with many backward glances, sad to leave, while so thrilled to have completed our quest to see our Lord and Saviour.

-The Magi

ECHOES

After the Manger

Matthew 2:13–20

Now when they [the Magi] had gone, behold, an angel of the Lord appeared to Joseph in a dream and said, 'Get up! Take the Child and His mother and flee to Egypt, and stay there until I tell you; for Herod is going to search for the Child to kill Him.'

So Joseph got up and took the Child and His mother while it was still night, and left for Egypt. He stayed there until the death of Herod: this happened so that what had been spoken by the Lord through the prophet would be fulfilled: *'Out of Egypt I called my Son.'*

Then when Herod saw that he had been tricked by the magi, he became very enraged, and sent men and killed all the boys who were in Bethlehem and all its vicinity who were two years old or under, according to the time which he had been determined from the magi.

Then what had been spoken through Jeremiah the prophet was fulfilled:

'A voice was heard in Ramah,
Weeping and great mourning,

Rachel weeping for her children;
And she refused to be comforted,
Because they are no more.'

But when Herod died, behold, an angel of the Lord appeared in a dream to Joseph in Egypt, and said, 'Get up, take the Child and His mother, and go to the land of Israel; for those who sought the Child's life are dead.'

Luke 2:39–40

...they returned to Galilee, to their own city of Nazareth. Now the Child continued to grow and become strong, increasing in wisdom; and the favour of God was upon Him.

VOICE 11

JOHN THE BAPTIST: 'His name is John'

'Andrew bar Jonah, I'm sure you have heard my story before, haven't you?' I say as I gather firewood one night with my keenest disciple.

'Well, yes,' replies Andrew. 'But Rabbi John, I've only heard it in bits, mostly what other people have told me. I would very much like to hear the whole story from the one whom it's about. After all, it's your story, Rabbi, and no one can tell it better than you, can they?'

'All right,' I say. 'Get the rest of my disciples here. We'll build the fire, and we can all have a meal together. Then I'll go over it all again, just this once more.'

After the meal, I begin. 'So, you know all about how Zechariah, my abba, was serving in the Temple at the time of the incense offering, when an angel appeared to him. The angel said that he would have a son whom he was to call John.

'Relatives and neighbours came to my circumcision. You see, I was famous even as a baby. They all expected me to be called Zechariah after my abba.

Then Elizabeth, my ima, spoke up and said, "No! His name must be John."

'They objected because it was the custom for the eldest son to continue the father's name. "But you have no relatives with that name!" they said. So, they signalled to my abba to find out what he would have me called.

'He asked for a writing tablet and wrote, "His name is John."

'They were all shocked, but there was more to come. At that moment, my abba's speech returned, and he gave praise to our LORD Adonai. Now our companions weren't just shocked, they were scared. Afterwards, they started to spread the news all about the Judean hill country. All who heard it wondered who on earth I was going to be. It was clear that the power of God was upon me.

'My abba started to prophecy, saying that the LORD had come to help His people Israel by providing a Saviour descended from his servant, David.

'He took me in his hands, held me up to God, and said,

> You, my child, will be called a prophet of the Most High God.
> You will go ahead of the Lord to prepare his road for him,
> To tell his people that they will be saved by having their sins forgiven.[20]

---

[20] Luke 1:76 -77 GNBUK

'He went on to bless the LORD, saying,

> Our God is merciful and tender.
> He will cause the bright dawn of salvation to rise on us
> and to shine from heaven on all those who live in the dark shadow of death,
> to guide our steps into the path of peace.[21]

'I had a lovely time growing up in Ein Kerem. I was my parents' darling, for they had waited so long for me. But they were not young, rather, well stricken in years. They decided to put me in the care of the desert people, so I could grow up safely protected and be instructed in the things of our God. After my Bar Mitzva, they took me to that community where I lived until recently.'

'What was it like to live with that group?' asks Andrew. 'I've heard that they are very strict and live by every tiny detail of the Law of Moses.'

'Yes, it's true. They come down very hard on anyone who breaks their precepts. There are punishments for sin and immorality, so they have a system of ritual washings and penance. That's all tied in with their expectation of the coming of the Messiah, to set our people free and bring in a new Davidic reign.

'My parents never told them that I am to announce the coming of that Messiah and to take on the mantle of the prophet Elijah in preparing His path. I think that was wise. They both wept as they left me, but even

---

[21] Luke 1:78-79 GNBUK

though it was hard, they knew it was the right thing to do. They were good people who loved the LORD Adonai and were able to end their days happy, knowing that they had fulfilled God's will. It was not long after that they went to Abraham's bosom.'

-John the Baptist

ECHOES

Luke 1:68-69, 76-80 (NIV)

Zechariah's Prophecy

'Praise be to the Lord, the God of Israel,
because he has come to his people and redeemed them.
He has raised up a horn of salvation for us
in the house of his servant David.'

'And you, my child, will be called a prophet of the Most High;
for you will go on before the Lord to prepare the way for him,
to give his people the knowledge of salvation
through the forgiveness of their sins,
because of the tender mercy of our God,
by which the rising sun will come to us from heaven
to shine on those living in darkness and in the shadow of death,
to guide our feet into the path of peace.'

And the child grew and became strong in spirit; and he lived in the wilderness until he appeared publicly to Israel.

VOICE 12

JOHN THE BAPTIST: Proclaiming Christ

'Life was not always easy in the desert,' I continue, as I glance at my band of faithful followers. 'We even had to make our own clothes from what we could get. See, my tunic is made of camel's hair and my belt of leather. Food was always in short supply. Sometimes I've even eaten locusts and wild honey. On the other hand, it was wonderful because I was taught the Scriptures and they prepared me to fulfil my calling – to prepare the way for the Messiah who is to come. Now, that time has arrived!'

'You mean He is here? Have you seen Him?' Andrew asks.

'No, not yet, but I know He has come. The LORD Adonai has told me how I will know Him. When He is here, the Holy Spirit will come on Him and anoint Him for His ministry. When I see that happen, I will know it's Him. But I am tired now, so let's get some sleep. Tomorrow we will go again to the Jordan, preach our good news, and continue baptizing those who repent.'

The next day, I take my little band to the river at Bethabara, and I call on the people to repent.

'Prepare yourselves for the coming of Messiah. I urge you to turn away from your sins, be baptized, and then God will forgive you.'

I tell them to change their lives and act accordingly, showing that they have left their evil ways by loving the LORD Adonai, and by loving their neighbours as they love themselves.

Ordinary people start to repent. Even tax collectors and soldiers are baptised, calling on God to forgive them and changing how they live. Of course, there is opposition from the Levites, the Sadducees and the Pharisees, who think themselves already righteous. They think they do not need to improve what is to them, quite perfect!

They ask me if I am the Coming One. I reply, 'No, I've told you. I am not the Messiah, nor Elijah, nor the Prophet. The Messiah is so much better than me, that I am not even worthy to undo his sandals.'

I am the voice of one shouting in the desert, to prepare the path of the Lord, just as the prophet Isaiah said:

> In the desert prepare the way for the LORD;
> make straight in the wilderness a highway for our God.[22]

I rebuke the leaders of Israel. 'You brood of vipers, who told you to escape from the punishment God is

[22] Isaiah 40:3 paraphrase

about to send? Bring out fruit that will show that you have turned from your sins. Just being descendants of Abraham will not do; that won't save you from punishment. The axe is already laid to the root of the trees. Bring forth good fruit or be cut down and thrown into the fire.'[23]

They don't like it!

Finally, the day comes when I see Jesus coming down to the Jordan. I yell, 'This is the Lamb of God! He takes away the sin of the world.'[24]

Jesus wants me to baptize Him. I know it is me that needs to be baptized by Him, but He insists I permit it now to fulfil all righteousness. So I plunge him into the water.

As He comes up out of the water, the sky seems to open. I see the Spirit of God come down like a dove, alighting on Him and filling His whole being.

A voice from heaven calls aloud to him, 'You are My own dear Son, My beloved One. I am delighted in You.'[25]

The very next day, I stand with Andrew bar Jonah and John, son of Zebedee, as Jesus comes past alone. I tell them, 'Look! There is the Lamb of God!'

They turn to follow him, then hesitate, for I know they want to stay with me as well.

---

[23] Luke 3:7-9 paraphrased

[24] John 1:29 paraphrased

[25] Luke 3:22 paraphrased

So, I tell them, 'Go. He must increase, while I must decrease.'[26] Then they go after Him.

Indeed, Jesus is the future. It is my joy to prepare for Him. Nevertheless, tears well up in my eyes as they depart.

Jesus turns. He asks them what they want.

They reply, 'Rabbi, where are you staying?'

He answers, 'Come and see.' And they go along with Him.[27]

Now I must find others to follow Him. In a way, my job is complete, just as my father Zechariah declared, when he was filled with the Holy Spirit. My parents were faithful to God, setting the scene for the day when I was able to announce to the world that Jesus is the LORD'S Anointed One, setting out on His mission to redeem the world.

Now I echo my abba's words:

> Let us praise the Lord, the God of Israel! He has come to the help of his people and has set them free. He has provided for us a mighty Saviour, a descendant of His servant David. He promised through his holy prophets long ago that He would save us from our enemies, from the power of all those who hate us.[28]

-John the Baptist

---

[26] John 3:30 paraphrased

[27] John 3: 35-39 paraphrased

[28] Luke 1:68-71 paraphrased

ECHOES

Isaiah 40:1–2 (GNBUK)

'Comfort My people,' says our God. 'Comfort them!'
Encourage the people of Jerusalem.
Tell them they have suffered long enough, and their sins are now forgiven.

John 1:26–27, 29–32 (GNBUK)

John answered, 'I baptize with water, but among you stands the one you do not know. He is coming after me, but I am not good enough even to untie his sandals.'

The next day John saw Jesus coming to him, and said, 'There is the Lamb of God, who takes away the sin of the world! This is the one I was talking about when I said, 'A man is coming after me, but he is greater than I am, because he existed before I was born.'

Psalm 92:13–14 (GNBUK)

(Of John’s parents)

They are like trees planted in the house of the LORD,
that flourish in the Temple of our God,
that still bear fruit in old age
and are always green and strong.

GOING FURTHER

There is something important that you need to know: **God loves you! Yes, He loves you!**

He created mankind to have fellowship with His sons and daughters.

It's what He still wants.

No, your God does not hate you, nor does He condemn you for the mistakes and failures you have committed. What He does hate is the sin that has separated His sons and daughters from Him. That is what has brought such suffering on you, and such sorrow to Him. It took away your eternal life in God and brought death and condemnation for all eternity.

But He has done something about it.

God has sent His Son, Jesus Christ of Nazareth, to restore our fellowship.

> For God so loved the world, that He gave His only Son, so that everyone who believes in Him will not perish, but have eternal life. For God did not send the Son into the world to judge the world, but so that the world might be saved through Him.
>
> **John 3:16-17**

That is why Jesus came from His eternal throne in Glory to a dirty old stable in Bethlehem, why He lived a life of love and service, and why He eventually died on that cross at Calvary. There, Jesus took all our sin and condemnation on Himself and paid for it with His own blood, like a lamb led to the slaughter.

On the third day, He rose again, resurrected by the power of the Holy Spirit, to give new life to all those who call on His Name and to bring us back into fellowship with God as the sons and daughters He always wanted.

So, what do you need to do to receive all God's blessings, to receive new life, to become His child, and be saved to have all the joy and peace with your Father God?

Paul put it like this:

> ... if you confess with your mouth Jesus as Lord, and believe in your heart that God raised Him from the dead, you will be saved.
>
> For with the heart a person believes, resulting in righteousness, and with the mouth he confesses, resulting in salvation.
>
> **Romans 10:9-10**

All you have to do is believe in what Jesus did for you. Ask Him to give you His salvation. Receive His gift of new life and say, 'Thank You'.

It just might be that you are not familiar with praying, or you may not be confident about what to say. So here is a prayer you can use if you wish.

Prayer

Lord Jesus, I believe that You are our Saviour, that You died on the cross for all my sins and failures.
I ask You to forgive me and make me clean in the eyes of God by washing me in Your precious blood.
I believe that You were raised from the dead and that You give me your righteousness.
I declare now that You are my Saviour and my Lord.
Thank you for saving me. Amen.

If you have just prayed this, that's wonderful!

Congratulations!
Welcome to the Family.
Hallelujah!
Thank You, Jesus!

-Alick

Acknowledgements

My first and ultimate thanks go (of course) to our Lord God for the original idea to write down these thoughts from the point of view of some participants in Jesus' story.

From a 'spoken word' challenge by Hannah, and a request by Glyn and Veronique for a life group presentation about Zechariah, came the idea to chronicle the events of Jesus' birth. So, *Voices* began.

My special thanks go to Joy Margetts who encouraged me to persevere, who edited my first attempts, suggested ways to improve the text and was always so positive. *Voices* might have gone no further than my computer but for her.

Kingdom Story Writers have been an inspiration. They are a growing force in promoting excellent faith-filled literature which believers and our society need so much. My grateful thanks to them for putting up with me.

I am so grateful to Natasha Woodcraft for her editing and formatting of my work. Her sympathetic corrections and suggestions lift my efforts to a new level. Thank you so much.

Also thanks to Natasha Woodcraft and Josh Willink at pexels.com for the gorgeous cover design. It is magnificent.

More than anyone else, I want to thank my lovely wife, Lynn. She has encouraged me, supported me and shown enduring patience, especially when 'I just have to finish this' often results in keeping my dinner warm.

Finally, if these jottings bless anyone, it is all due to our lovely Jesus who gave His all for us.

Thank you, Lord!

-Alick

About the Author

Alick H Ford taught Science and Maths in senior schools and further education for 40 years before leaving teaching and moving to the 'top lefthand corner' of Wales, with his dear wife, Lynn.

He was a founding member of Goleudy Community Church, Criccieth, teaching God's Word to empower believers to live the abundant life bought for them by our Saviour, Jesus.

Printed in Great Britain
by Amazon

57050288R00056